CARNIVORES

BY
S.L. HAMILTON

A&D Xtreme
An imprint of Abdo Publishing | www.abdopublishing.com

Printed in the United States of America, North Mankato, MN.
092017
012018

 THIS BOOK CONTAINS
RECYCLED MATERIALS

Editor: John Hamilton
Graphic Design: Sue Hamilton
Cover Design: Candice Keimig and Pakou Vang
Cover Photo: iStock
Interior Photos & Illustrations: AP-pgs 28-29; Deposit Photos-Pgs 22-23; iStock-pgs 1, 2-3, 10-11 & 30-31; Reuters-pgs 12-13; Science Source-pgs 6-7 & 8-9; Shutterstock-pgs 4-5, 14-15, 16-17, 18-19, 20-21, 24-25 & 32; Vladimir Bondar & GEAL/CCID/Museu da Lourinha-pgs 26-27.

Publisher's Cataloging-in-Publication Data

Names: Hamilton, S.L., author.
Title: Carnivores / by S.L. Hamilton.
Description: Minneapolis, Minnesota : Abdo Publishing, 2018. | Series: Xtreme Dinosaurs | Includes online resources and index.
Identifiers: LCCN 2017946706 | ISBN 9781532112935 (lib.bdg.) | ISBN 9781532150791 (ebook)
Subjects: LCSH: Carnivorous animals, Fossil--Juvenile literature. | Prehistoric animals--Juvenile literature. | Dinosaurs--Juvenile literature. | Paleontology--Juvenile literature.
Classification: DDC 567.912--dc23
LC record available at https://lccn.loc.gov/2017946706

CONTENTS

MEAT EATERS

Carnivores, or meat-eating dinosaurs, lived during the Mesozoic era. Also known as theropods, they died out 65 million years ago. Their fossils tell us these bloodthirsty hunters and scavengers were made for eating animals and fish.

Albertosaurus
(Alberta Lizard)

XTREME FACT – Only about 35 percent of dinosaurs were carnivores (meat eaters) or omnivores (meat and plant eaters). Most dinosaurs were herbivores (plant eaters).

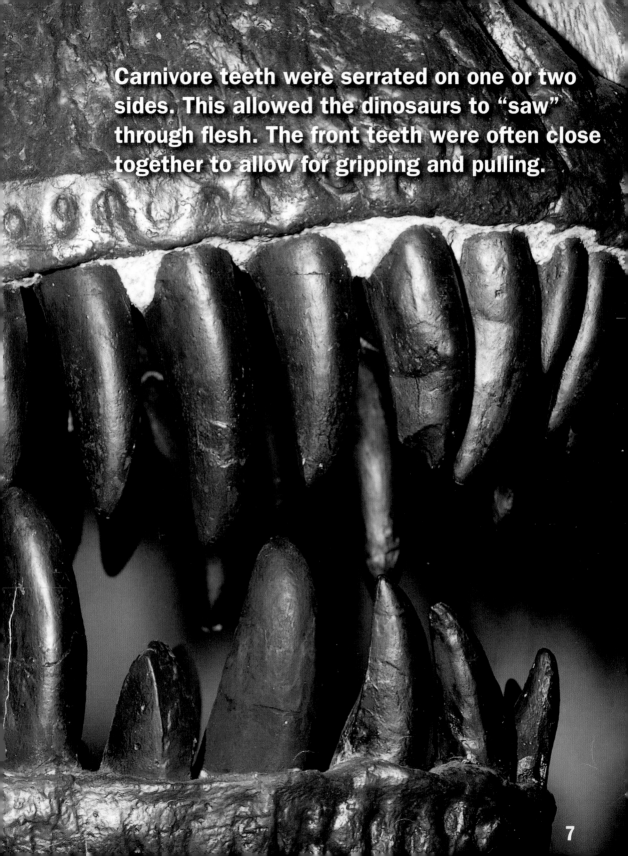

Carnivore teeth were serrated on one or two sides. This allowed the dinosaurs to "saw" through flesh. The front teeth were often close together to allow for gripping and pulling.

CLAWS

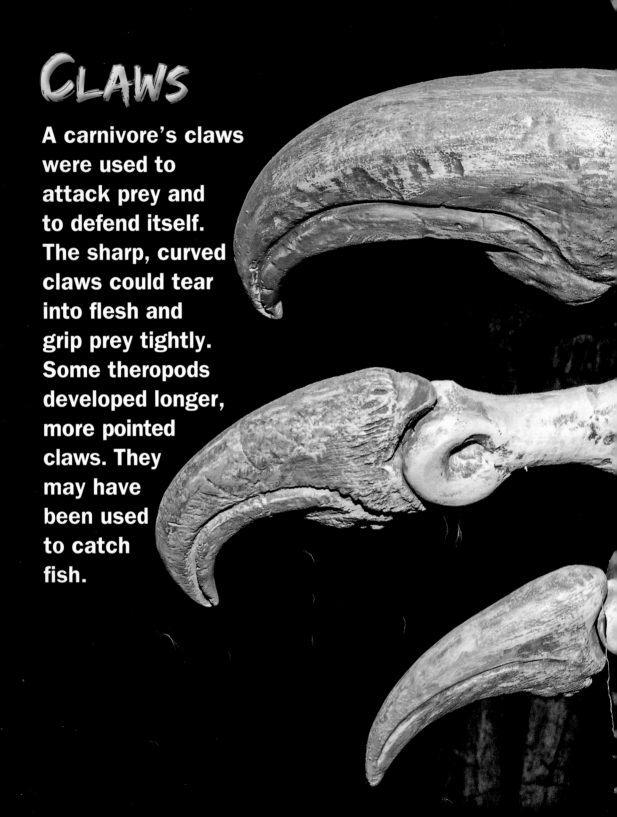

A carnivore's claws were used to attack prey and to defend itself. The sharp, curved claws could tear into flesh and grip prey tightly. Some theropods developed longer, more pointed claws. They may have been used to catch fish.

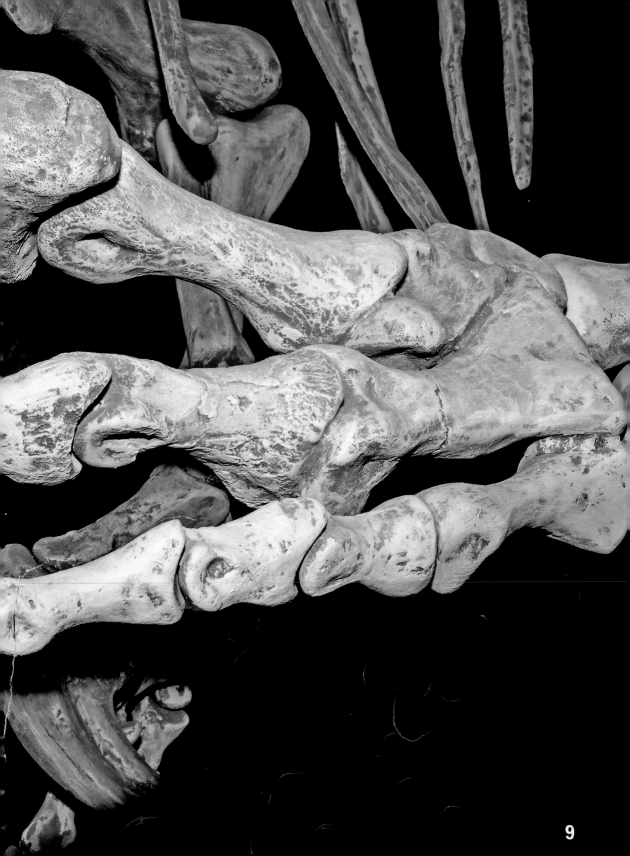

EYESIGHT

Meat-eating dinosaurs likely had excellent eyesight. Carnivores' eye sockets were quite large compared to their whole skull. Large eyes allow in lots of light. Lots of light means better sight. Like today's birds of prey, theropods were probably very good at spotting their next meal. Many may have had good enough vision to hunt at night.

XTREME FACT – Each huge eye of a Tyrannosaurus rex *was about the size of a tennis ball, 3 inches (8 cm) in diameter.*

SENSE OF SMELL

Carnivores probably had an excellent sense of smell. Scientists have studied the olfactory bulb area of dinosaur skulls. This is the area of the brain that sorts out scents.

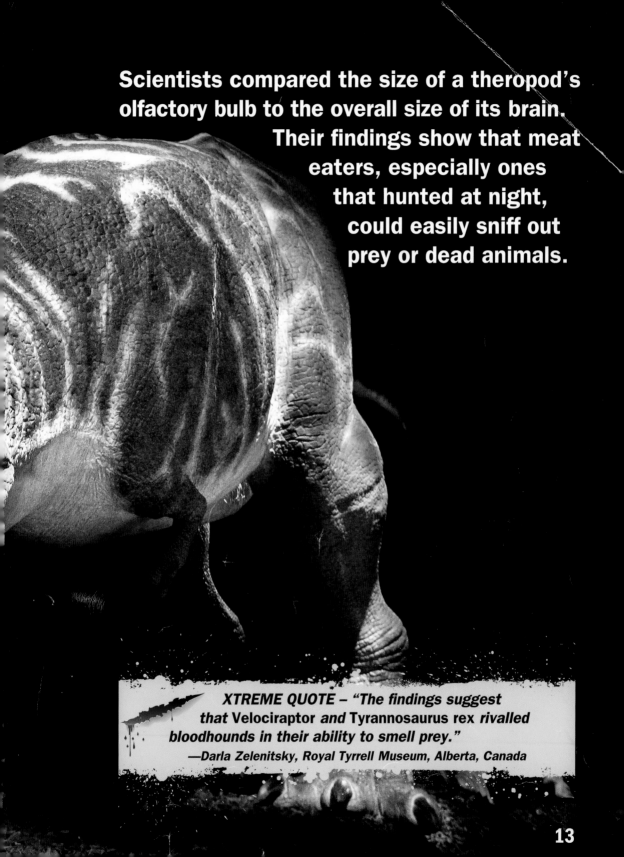

Scientists compared the size of a theropod's olfactory bulb to the overall size of its brain. Their findings show that meat eaters, especially ones that hunted at night, could easily sniff out prey or dead animals.

XTREME QUOTE – *"The findings suggest that* Velociraptor *and* Tyrannosaurus rex *rivalled bloodhounds in their ability to smell prey."*
—*Darla Zelenitsky, Royal Tyrrell Museum, Alberta, Canada*

LARGEST CARNIVORES

Spinosaurus was the largest carnivorous dinosaur. It lived in North Africa about 112 million to 97 million years ago. No complete *Spinosaurus* skeleton exists. Scientists guess that the huge theropod grew up to 59 feet (18 m) long.

Spinosaurus
(Spine Lizard)

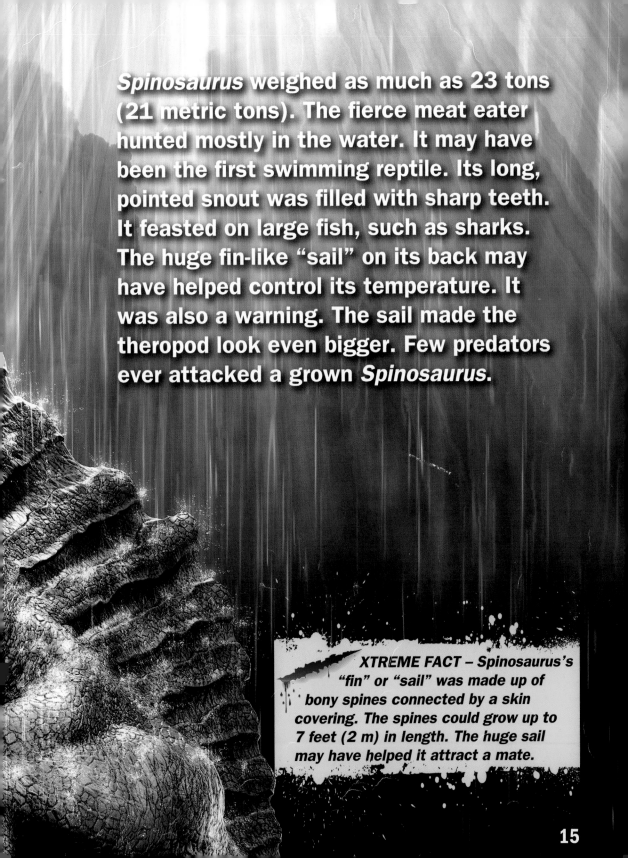

Spinosaurus weighed as much as 23 tons (21 metric tons). The fierce meat eater hunted mostly in the water. It may have been the first swimming reptile. Its long, pointed snout was filled with sharp teeth. It feasted on large fish, such as sharks. The huge fin-like "sail" on its back may have helped control its temperature. It was also a warning. The sail made the theropod look even bigger. Few predators ever attacked a grown *Spinosaurus*.

XTREME FACT – *Spinosaurus's* "fin" or "sail" was made up of bony spines connected by a skin covering. The spines could grow up to 7 feet (2 m) in length. The huge sail may have helped it attract a mate.

Gigantosaurus grew up to 43 feet (13 m) long and weighed as much as 14 tons (12.7 metric tons). It lived about 99.6 to 97 million years ago.

Gigantosaurus
(Giant Southern Lizard)

Gigantosaurus roamed modern-day South America. It hunted large herbivore dinosaurs. The giant theropod had sharp, serrated teeth, but not a very powerful jaw. Scientists believe the teeth were used to repeatedly bite or slice into its prey until its victim died.

XTREME FACT – No complete Gigantosaurus skeleton has ever been found. Scientists guess its size based on the fossil bones that have been discovered.

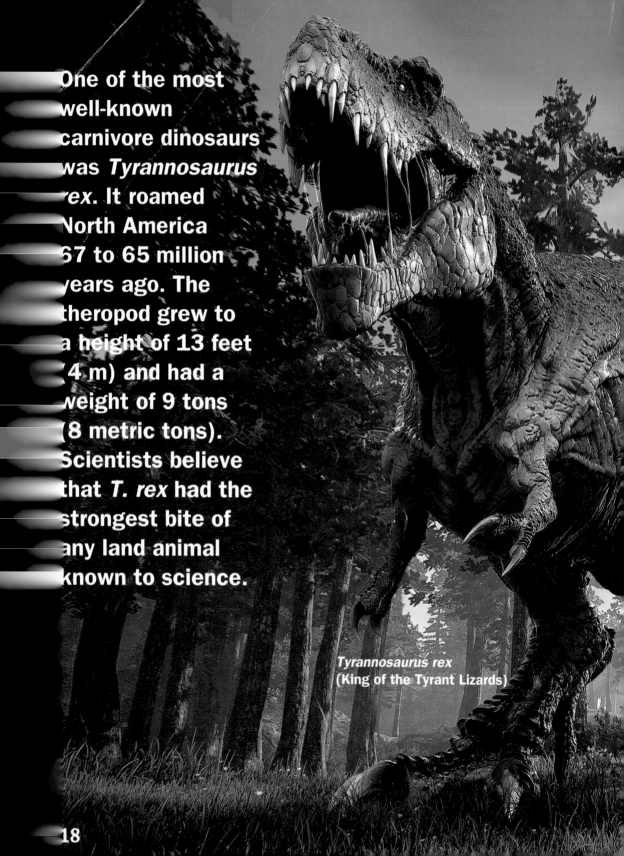

One of the most well-known carnivore dinosaurs was *Tyrannosaurus rex*. It roamed North America 67 to 65 million years ago. The theropod grew to a height of 13 feet (4 m) and had a weight of 9 tons (8 metric tons). Scientists believe that *T. rex* had the strongest bite of any land animal known to science.

Tyrannosaurus rex
(King of the Tyrant Lizards)

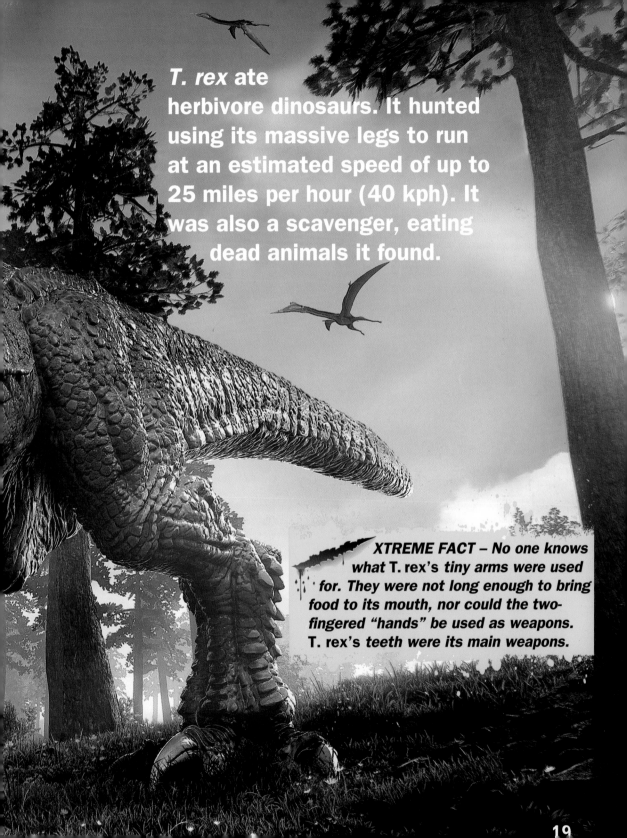

T. rex ate herbivore dinosaurs. It hunted using its massive legs to run at an estimated speed of up to 25 miles per hour (40 kph). It was also a scavenger, eating dead animals it found.

XTREME FACT – No one knows what T. rex's tiny arms were used for. They were not long enough to bring food to its mouth, nor could the two-fingered "hands" be used as weapons. T. rex's teeth were its main weapons.

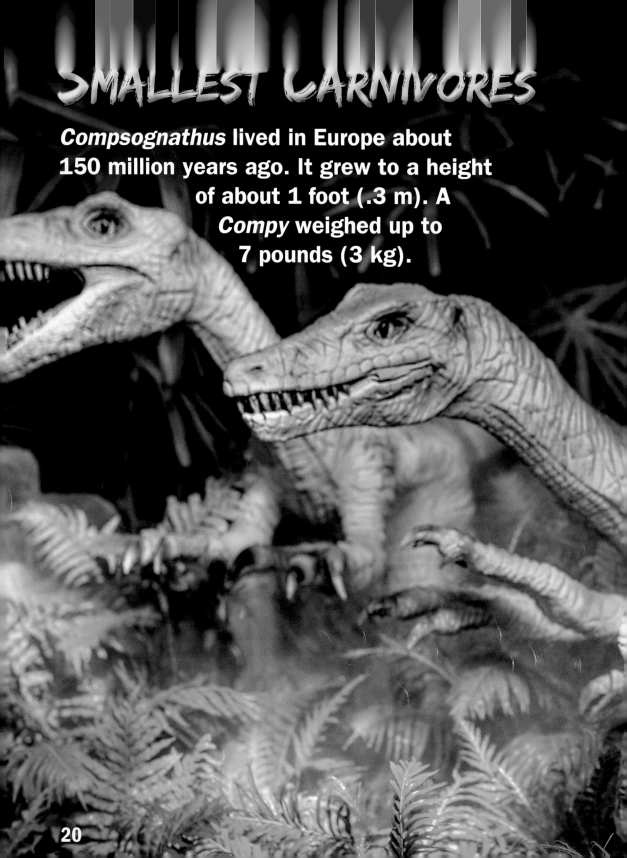

Smallest Carnivores

Compsognathus lived in Europe about 150 million years ago. It grew to a height of about 1 foot (.3 m). A *Compy* weighed up to 7 pounds (3 kg).

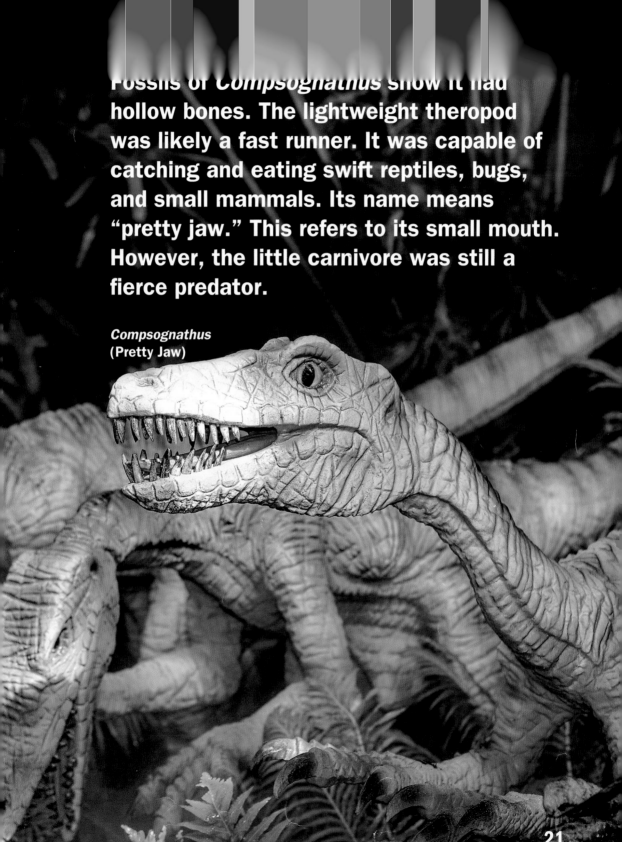

Fossils of *Compsognathus* show it had hollow bones. The lightweight theropod was likely a fast runner. It was capable of catching and eating swift reptiles, bugs, and small mammals. Its name means "pretty jaw." This refers to its small mouth. However, the little carnivore was still a fierce predator.

Compsognathus
(Pretty Jaw)

Dilong paradoxus was one of the smallest carnivore dinosaurs. It grew to a height of 3 feet (.9 m) and weighed about 25 pounds (11 kg). It roamed today's China 125 to 146 million years ago.

Dilong paradoxus
(Emperor Dragon)

Dilong had long arms ending in three-fingered clawed hands. The nimble fingers allowed it to hunt and hold its meals of small lizards, birds, and mammals.

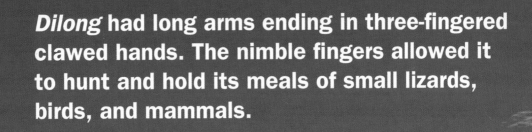

XTREME FACT – *There are several species in the tyrannosaur family. Dilong is the smallest tyrannosaur ever discovered. It may have been covered in small feathers to help keep it warm.*

FASTEST CARNIVORES

Nanotyrannus lancensis is believed to have been one of the fastest carnivore dinosaurs. It lived in today's North America, about 68 to 66 million years ago.

Nanotyrannus lancensis
(Dwarf Tyrant)

XTREME QUOTE – *"Of all the dinosaurs, Nanotyrannus is the one that I would least like to be chased by. Taking the characteristically long legs of tyrannosaurs to the extreme, Nanotyrannus had the stride to leave all other big carnivores in the dust."* —Dr. Scott Persons, paleontologist, University of Alberta

The "dwarf tyrant" grew to about 6.5 feet (2 m) tall. This small tyrannosaur evolved its long legs, big stride, and speed in order to catch prey that its larger cousin, *Tyrannosaurus rex*, could not.

NESTING

It is rare to find fossilized nests and eggs. However, studies of 150- to 90-million-year-old dinosaur eggs show that many theropods made above-ground nests. It is believed that some carnivorous dinosaurs protected their offspring. They may have lived and hunted as a family.

A theropod dinosaur at its nest.

XTREME FACT – No one knew for sure if dinosaurs laid eggs or had live births until a nest of fossilized eggs was found in Mongolia in 1923.

EXTINCTION

Dinosaurs lived for about 165 million years. However, a terrible event occurred 65 million years ago that killed the great reptiles.

XTREME QUOTE – "If all of Earth time from the very beginning of the dinosaurs to today were compressed into 365 days (1 calendar year), the dinosaurs appeared January 1 and became extinct the third week of September."

—USGS (United States Geological Survey)

Scientists believe an extreme event changed the dinosaurs' world. Perhaps a huge asteroid struck the Earth and changed the climate. Maybe volcanoes began erupting. It's possible diseases killed the dinosaurs. Fossil hunters continue to search for clues as to what brought extinction to the powerful reptiles that once ruled the Earth.

GLOSSARY

BIRDS OF PREY
Birds that eat meat, such as eagles, hawks, or owls. Birds of prey are also known as raptors.

EXTINCT
When every member of a specific living thing has died. Dinosaurs are extinct.

FOSSILS
The preserved remains or imprints of prehistoric animals or plants in stone.

HERBIVORES
Animals that eat only plants as food.

MESOZOIC ERA
A time in Earth's history from about 245 million years ago to 65 million years ago. Dinosaurs roamed the Earth at this time. This era is made up of the Triassic, Jurassic, and Cretaceous periods.

OMNIVORES
Animals that eat both plants and meat.

PALEONTOLOGIST
A person who studies prehistoric fossil plants and animals.

PREDATOR

An animal that hunts, kills, and eats other animals.

SCAVENGERS

Creatures that eat what they can find, including dead and dying prey.

SERRATED

Notched like the edge of a saw. Modern-day sharks have serrated teeth. This allows the carnivore to rip off big chunks of meat.

SNOUT

The nose and mouth areas of an animal.

THEROPODS

Dinosaurs that walked on two legs and usually ate meat. These carnivores ranged in size from small, turkey-sized dinosaurs to huge monsters as tall as one-and-a-half telephone poles.

ONLINE RESOURCES

Booklinks
NONFICTION NETWORK
FREE! ONLINE NONFICTION RESOURCES

To learn more about Xtreme Dinosaurs, visit abdobooklinks.com. These links are routinely monitored and updated to provide the most current information available.

INDEX